This book belongs to

_____

Written by Stephen Barnett
Illustrated by Rosie Brooks

Contents

Cooking with mum 3

Our new bike 13

In the tent 23

New words 31

What did you learn? 32

About this book

Childhood is about learning and the stories here recount special events which bring new understanding to the child. Word lists at the back of the book and questions related to the stories further enhance the reader's enjoyment.

Cooking with mum

Once a week my mum and I take the flour from the cupboard, the eggs and milk from the fridge, the bowls from the bench, the spoons from the drawer and we ...

make a cake!

'Come on, you can crack the eggs if you like and stir them into the flour,' says my mother.

Cracking the eggs is fun but sometimes I crack the shell too hard and bits of the egg fly everywhere!

Then we add the milk, a little sugar and some baking powder and

maybe a little chocolate.

Next, we stir the mixture until it's smooth. Then we pour it into a cake tin. When the oven is hot, mum puts the cake in. We clean the dishes while we wait for the cake to bake.

I always eat what is left in the mixing bowl. I use a spoon and lick it clean! Mum says that this is my reward for helping.

When the cake is ready to eat, mum calls the family together. Everyone smiles and they always say, 'Oh, this is the best cake ever!'

Our new bike

I needed a new bike. My old bike was now too small for me, and my little sister Jenny had taken it over as her bike. I asked my parents how soon we could go shopping to buy a new bike.

One day mum said to me, 'Tomorrow we'll get a bike for you.' I jumped up and down with excitement. Then dad said, 'But new bikes cost a lot of money so we'll look at an old bike instead. Dad gave me a smile, 'Don't you worry, it will be the best bike in the world!'

I was a little sad. I had been dreaming about having a shiny, new bike. How could an old bike be any better?

I was very quiet the next morning as we got ready to go to the market.

At the market the man who ran the bicycle stall showed us lots and lots of old bikes. Some had rust on them, some had flat tyres, some had broken seats.

Now and then dad asked me to sit on one of the bikes to check that it was the right size. Finally, dad said, 'This is the one! It's just right!'

I looked at the bike. I couldn't believe he would choose this one. The bike's paint was scratched and it was missing its light. It had rust and the wheels were covered in oil and dust. During the next few days, mum and dad worked on the bike out in the shed at the back of our house.

Then, one morning at breakfast dad said, 'Was that a knock at the door, Kevin? Could you have a look, please, to see if anyone's there?' I walked to the front door and opened it. There was no one there. I pushed the door open further and looked along the porch.

There was the most amazing bike I had ever seen! It was painted dark blue and green. It had a new shiny black seat, a basket, silver wheels and new tyres. It was beautiful! I rushed inside and hugged mum and dad and then went back and took the bike for a ride in the front lawn. Around and around I went. I felt wonderful. Best of all, dad had painted on the side of the bike in very small letters, 'The best bike in the world'. It really was!

In the tent

My friend Alan and I had been playing a game of marbles for a long time and I was getting tired of it.
'Let's do something else', I said.

'Like what?' asked Alan.
We lay back on the grass and started thinking. We needed to find something new and different.

'I've got it', I said as I stood up. 'Let's go camping!'
'Where are we going to do that?' asked Alan. 'Our parents won't let us go to the forest by ourselves.

'What about right here?' I said, pointing around the garden. 'We can set up the tent in the far corner of the garden under this tree and it will be like we are in the forest.'
'Good idea, said Alan. 'And if we get hungry, your kitchen is close by!'

For the next hour we worked hard putting up the tent. We brought out blankets and pillows from my bedroom. We made sandwiches and filled up water bottles. We got torches from Alan's house to use in the dark.

At last we were ready. My parents came to see what we had done.
'You boys have done a good job with this,' my dad said as he looked inside the tent.
'Have you got enough to eat?' asked mum. 'What do you think, Alan? Would you like some cake as well?'
Alan smiled and said yes.

At midnight, it started to rain. At first it was exciting but after a while we started to feel a little wet. The rain was too heavy for the tent and it was starting to leak!
'Come on! Let us get out of here!' said Alan.
We ran back into the house, dragging the blankets and the pillows with us. Mum was already at the door.
'Inside, boys, quick!' she called out. She gave us towels to dry ourselves.

New words

amazing	fridge
baking powder	instead
basket	leak
bench	marble
camp	market
cost	mixture
crack	oven
cupboard	porch
different	reward
enough	rust
everyone	scratch
excitement	stall
flat tyres	torch
flour	

What did you learn?

Cooking with mum

Where were the spoons kept?

What were they making?

What did the family say about the cake?

In the tent

What was the name of the friend?

What game were they playing?

What happened to the tent when it rained?

Our new bike

Name the boy who needed a new bike?

Where did they buy the bike from?

What colour was the bike painted?